'I AM...'

'I AM...'

Six studies in John's Gospel
for groups

TONY KIDD

SCRIPTURE UNION

Scripture Union, 207–209 Queensway, Bletchley, MK2 2EB, England.

© Tony Kidd 1997

First published 1997

ISBN 1 85999 176 9

British Library Cataloguing-in-Publication Data
A catalogue record for this book is available from the British Library.

Cover design by Rafale Design.
Cover illustration by Sally Elson.
Internal illustrations by Helen Gale
Printed and bound in Great Britain by Cox & Wyman Ltd, Reading.

CONTENTS

FOREWORD

Tony Kidd manages to bring his proven gifts as a teacher and pastor to the written page. Those who do this course, carved out of Tony's own pastoral experience, will find themselves taught the essence of the Christian faith. He opens up the meanings of the pictures Jesus used to describe himself, he applies them to our lives imaginatively and demonstrates clearly their significance. I warmly commend this course. It will open eyes to see Jesus more clearly and to love him more dearly.

Rt Revd James Jones, Bishop of Hull

INTRODUCTION

Jesus said, 'I am the vine, you are the branches.'

What does it mean to be grafted into Jesus, the vine? What does it mean when he talks about being bread or light, or when he says 'I am the good shepherd' and 'I am the way and the truth, the resurrection and the life'? This course aims to deepen our understanding of the significance of these claims, and to encourage us to ask not only 'Who is Jesus?' but 'Who am I?'

The course has been written primarily for use by groups, although it may also be helpful to individuals. A group of six to ten people is ideal. Group members may like to appoint a leader, or take it in turns over the six weeks to be responsible for facilitating the group and keeping to time. Allow between one-and-a-half and two hours for each session. Suggested timings for the specific sections are:

Way in ....10–15 minutes   Response ...15–20 minutes
Bible ....20–30 minutes   Prayer ....10–20 minutes
Life ....5–10 minutes

The songs for each session can be found in *Let's Praise!* (LP), *Mission Praise* (MP, combined words edition), *Spring Harvest Praise 1996* (SHP), *Songs & Hymns of Fellowship* (SHF, integrated words edition), and *Songs of Fellowship* (SOF). There are also suggestions for music to be played when leading into times of prayer or during the meditations.

The meditations may be approached in three ways:

- You may like to read them on your own silently or, if no one else is near, out loud.

- If you are in a group, one person might read the meditation to the others. The passage should be read slowly, with pauses at appropriate points to allow time for people to take in the atmosphere and bring their imaginations into play.

- If the person reading to the group is feeling fairly confident, they might use the meditation as a basis for painting their own picture of the scene, pausing after each line to inject imagery or description.

An illustration appears near each meditation to provide a focus, but you may like to bring in an appropriate object such as a loaf of bread (session 1) or a lighted candle (session 2). Other pictures, either photographs or prints of paintings, could also be used. Be creative in thinking up ways to bring interest and variety to each session.

> NOTE: At times of sharing, no one should feel obliged to say more than they want to, and individual privacy must always be respected. As a group, be sensitive to the possibility that some members may find parts of the sessions difficult. Providing support in such circumstances could be very helpful.

The pattern of prayer on pages 19–21 is designed for use each day during the course, and may be adapted to suit personal taste and practice. The daily readings form a natural part of the pattern of prayer.

The following are the readings for the three days before the first meeting:

Preparation	Day 1	Exodus 16:11–16, 31–33: Manna in the desert
	Day 2	Matthew 15:32–39: Feeding the four thousand
	Day 3	Luke 22:14–23: The last supper
Meeting	**Day 4**	**John 6:27–40: Jesus, the bread of life**

1

'I AM THE BREAD OF LIFE'

Aim

To think how we are fed spiritually.

Way in

ICEBREAKER

This is an optional activity to help you begin to get to know one another in the group. You may also find it a useful introduction to the theme of the course.

Using the phrase 'I am...', talk about yourself to your neighbour for no more than a minute or two, then listen while he/she does the same. Then take turns to introduce your neighbour to the group.

PREPARING

You may like to begin with some music to help you prepare to meet with God. For those who enjoy singing, the songs listed below reflect the theme of this first session. These are only suggestions: you may wish to choose your own.

Songs to sing

'Break Thou the Bread of Life', MP 64, SHF 46, SOF 50.
'Broken for me, broken for you', LP 18, MP 66, SOF 53.
'Father God, the Lord, Creator', MP 130.
'Hallelujah! Sing to Jesus', MP 207, SHF 151, SOF 153.
'I am the Bread of Life', MP 261, SHF 182, SOF 200.
'Just as I am', LP 101, MP 396, SHF 304, SOF 316.

Music to listen to

Mozart: Clarinet Concerto in A, K 622, 2nd movement
   (Adagio).
Adiemus: 'Cantus Insolitus', from *Songs of Sanctuary*.

Afterwards, have a time of prayer, perhaps leaving silence for
people to unburden themselves from the pressures of the day.
Allow opportunity for confession and thanksgiving.

WHAT WE EAT

What is the main ingredient in your diet (eg bread, rice, pasta) and
what are the various ways in which it can be used? Discuss this
together as a group.

Bible

Listen as the following Bible passage is read.

John 6:27–40

[Jesus said] 27 *'Do not work for the food that perishes, but
for the food that endures for eternal life, which the Son of
Man will give you. For it is on him that God the Father has
set his seal.'* 28 *Then they said to him, 'What must we do to
perform the works of God?'* 29 *Jesus answered them, 'This
is the work of God, that you believe in him whom he has
sent.'* 30 *So they said to him, 'What sign are you going to
give us then, so that we may see it and believe you? What
work are you performing?* 31 *Our ancestors ate the manna
in the wilderness; as it is written, "He gave them bread
from heaven to eat." '* 32 *Then Jesus said to them, 'Very
truly, I tell you, it was not Moses who gave you the bread
from heaven, but it is my Father who gives you the true
bread from heaven.* 33 *For the bread of God is that which
comes down from heaven and gives life to the world.'*
34 *They said to him, 'Sir, give us this bread always.'*
   35 *Jesus said to them, 'I am the bread of life. Whoever
comes to me will never be hungry, and whoever believes
in me will never be thirsty.* 36 *But I said to you that you*

have seen me and yet do not believe. [37] Everything that the Father gives me will come to me, and anyone who comes to me I will never drive away; [38] for I have come down from heaven, not to do my own will, but the will of him who sent me. [39] And this is the will of him who sent me, that I should lose nothing of all that he has given me, but raise it up on the last day. [40] This is indeed the will of my Father, that all who see the Son and believe in him may have eternal life; and I will raise them up on the last day.'

To the Jews of Jesus' time there were certain things that were so important, so fundamental to life, so much a part of a person's character, as to be *Kiddush*. This is literally 'bread and wine' but *Kiddush* actually means far more than that. If something is *Kiddush*, it embraces the whole idea behind the *Shabbat*, the meal eaten on a Friday by Jews preparing for the Sabbath. So *Kiddush* speaks of what it means to be a Jew, with all that this entails in terms of the history and culture of Israel, the chosen people. Something which is *Kiddush* is as important in defining the person as bread is in sustaining the body. It speaks of what is truly inside a person. So when Jesus claimed to be the 'bread of life' he was using very powerful words built on this Jewish concept.

Consider the following questions together:

- Do you belong to any groups or take part in any activities which help you express who you are?

- How important are a shared history and standards/values in helping you feel 'at home' with other people?

- Fellowship with other Christians is better when we are able to share in their experience. Can you suggest ways to make sharing easier?

Life

List your typical weekly activities under the appropriate heading of the four given below (social, physical, mental and spiritual). Rate each activity according to its importance, and make a note of the time spent on it. Total these for each of the four sections.

SUSTENANCE & GROWTH
(NOTE: In the rating below, 0 = least important and 10 = most important)

SOCIAL
How and where do you socialise (eg clubs, organisations, family)?

Activity	Rating (0–10)	Time spent
Total		

PHYSICAL
What do you do by way of exercise (eg sport, walking, gardening)?

Activity	Rating (0–10)	Time spent
Total		

MENTAL

What do you do that involves mental exercise, either in your work or leisure time?

Activity	Rating (0–10)	Time spent
Total		

SPIRITUAL

What time do you spend in Bible study, prayer, meditation or fellowship with other Christians?

Activity	Rating (0–10)	Time spent
Total		

Response

The questions below may help you analyse your response and reflect on it. You may consider them on your own or with one or two others. After a few minutes, if you wish, discuss your responses with the rest of the group.

- Looking at each category of activity in the 'Life' section, how do you feel about the breakdown of importance and time allocated to each one?

- Looking at each activity, how do you feel about the comparative importance of these?

- Are there areas where you feel, on reflection, that the balance is not right?

- Are there adjustments you would like to make as a result of this exercise?

Prayer

Use this time as an opportunity to share with others in the group anything that has been particularly significant for you during the session, and pray about it together.

Further reflection on the theme of this session will be aided by using the readings for the week and the pattern of prayer outlined on pages 19–21. You may wish to use these, along with the meditation and the words of praise, as a group, or individually throughout the week.

PRAISE (BASED ON PSALM 89)
Leader: O Lord, I will always sing of your constant love.
All: I will proclaim your faithfulness forever.
Leader: I know your love will last for all time.
All: I will proclaim your faithfulness forever.
Leader: I know your faithfulness is as permanent as the sky.
All: O Lord, I will proclaim your faithfulness forever.

> MEDITATION
> If I take this loaf within my hands —
> I hold the seed placed within the warm soil
> that trickles through my fingers as the crumbs fall.
> I hold the soft rain that seeks the seed and caresses it
> into new life with its gentle touch.
> I hold the sun's rays that warm the life
> and cause it to search upward to the source.
> I hold the green leaves and strong stalks

which yield a hundredfold.
I hold the flour and yeast in the baker's hands
and the oven's heat.
Then I have this bread to offer —
Fruit of the earth and the work of human hands.

PATTERN OF PRAYER
*You may like to use this pattern as a basis for your
daily prayers during the course.*

PRAISE AND THANKSGIVING
Spend a few moments thinking of the things you want to thank
God for, then offer them up to him in praise.

Based on Psalm 106:1
> *I praise you, Lord, and give you thanks,
> for you are good and your love endures forever.*

CONFESSION
Spend a few moments thinking of things you need to confess, ask-
ing for forgiveness.

Based on Psalm 51:1–2
> *Have mercy on me, O God,
> according to your unfailing love;*

according to your great compassion
blot out my transgressions.
Wash away all my iniquity
and cleanse me from all sin.

Based on John 8:11
Hear the words of forgiveness: 'Go, and sin no more.'

BIBLE
On each day when you are preparing for the next session, read the
Bible passage and spend time reflecting on it, making notes of any
feelings you experience.

or

On each day when you are reflecting on the last session, re-read
the key Bible passage for the session and make notes of any new
thoughts or feelings you have.

then

Use the reading for the day, or the meditation for the week past or
the week to come, and be still before God.

INTERCESSION
Bring to God:

*   any people or situations that you feel need his love
*   the other members of the group
*   your own needs

The Lord's Prayer
Our Father in heaven,
Hallowed be your name.
Your kingdom come,
your will be done on earth as it is in heaven.
Give us today our daily bread.
Forgive us our sins
as we forgive those who sin against us.
Lead us not into temptation

but deliver us from evil.
For the kingdom, the power and the glory are yours
now and forever. Amen.

> ### IN CLOSING
> Lord, let me go out in the peace of Jesus Christ.
> In his name I ask it. Amen.

Readings for the week

1 'I AM THE BREAD OF LIFE'

Reflection	Day 5	Isaiah 55: Invitation to the thirsty
	Day 6	Luke 15:11–24: The lost son
	Day 7	John 6:25–29: The food that lasts for eternal life

2 'I AM THE LIGHT OF THE WORLD'

Preparation	Day 1	Isaiah 60:1–12: The glory of the Lord (1)
	Day 2	Isaiah 60:1, 13–20: The glory of the Lord (2)
	Day 3	Psalm 27: 'The Lord is my light...'
Meeting	Day 4	**John 1:1–9; 8:12: 'I am the light of the world'**

2

'I AM THE LIGHT OF THE WORLD'

Aim

To see how we can be 'light' in the world.

Way in

If you wish to, share together the things that have particularly registered with you over the previous week during the times of reflection or preparation.

PREPARING

As before, you may like to begin with music. Then spend time praying together about the things you have already talked about. Allow some times of silence.

Songs to sing

'Jesus, you are the radiance', MP 391, SHF 298, SOF 312.
'Light has dawned', LP 111, MP 422, SOF 341.
'Lord, the light of your love', MP 445, SOF 362.
'O Thou who camest from above', MP 525, SOF 451.
'The earth was dark', LP 198, MP 643.
'Your word is a lamp', LP 232.

Music to listen to

Fauré: Requiem, Op 48, 'Pie Jesu'.
Beethoven: Piano Sonata No 14 in C sharp minor (Moonlight),
   1st movement.

ENLIGHTENMENT

What do you immediately think of when you hear the word 'light'? Discuss this as a group for a few minutes.

Bible

Listen to the following two Bible passages as they are read.

John 1:1–9

> [1] *In the beginning was the Word, and the Word was with God, and the Word was God.* [2] *He was in the beginning with God.* [3] *All things came into being through him, and without him not one thing came into being. What has come into being* [4] *in him was life, and the life was the light of all people.* [5] *The light shines in the darkness, and the darkness did not overcome it.*
>
> [6] *There was a man sent from God, whose name was John.* [7] *He came as a witness to testify to the light, so that all might believe through him.* [8] *He himself was not the light, but he came to testify to the light.* [9] *The true light, which enlightens everyone, was coming into the world.*

In Old Testament times light was thought of as bringing joy and blessing. The Jews believed that God was the source of all the benefits they received, and they expressed this with sayings such as 'The Lord is my light'. Indeed, Psalm 27 opens with David praising God for being his 'light and salvation'. So there was no difference between the provision God made by way of sunlight, and his spiritual leadership of their lives. The problem for us today is that we have separated God from his creation so that our spiritual lives are far harder to relate to the world in which we live. Yet the God who illuminates our spiritual path is the same as the one who enables the bulb to light when we press the switch.

John 8:12

12 *Again Jesus spoke to them, saying, 'I am the light of the world. Whoever follows me will never walk in darkness but will have the light of life.'*

As a group, discuss the following questions:

• Have you recently seen, heard or experienced something that has illuminated your awareness of God's presence in the world?

• Thinking about the passages that have just been read, and the verses below, what do you understand Jesus to mean when he refers to himself as 'the light of the world'?

John 3:16, 19

[Jesus said] 'For God so loved the world that he gave his only Son, so that everyone who believes in him may not perish but may have eternal life...

'And this is the judgement, that the light has come into the world, and people loved darkness rather than light because their deeds were evil.'

Matthew 5:14–16

[Jesus said] 'You are the light of the world. A city built on a hill cannot be hid. No one after lighting a lamp puts it under the bushel basket, but on the lampstand, and it gives light to all in the house. In the same way, let your light shine before others, so that they may see your good works and give glory to your Father in heaven.'

You may find that the following four questions help you to explore what it means to be 'light in the world'.

SHINING EXAMPLE?
Who has 'shone' in your life (ie has been a constant,
intermittent, bright or gentle presence)?

Do you see yourself as a 'light' for others (eg as a
leader, a companion, a friend)?

A LIGHT GROWING DIM?

*Have you ever felt let down when you needed someone
to be a light shining for you?*

*Do you sometimes feel the need to 'recharge your
batteries'? If so, how might you go about this?*

NOTE: As a group be sensitive to the possibility that
some members may find these questions difficult (for
example, because they have recently been let down).
Providing support in such circumstances could be
very helpful.

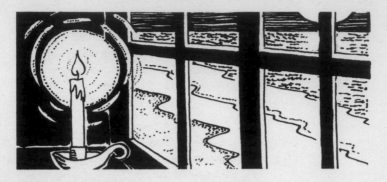

Response

Share your findings with the group.

Prayer

Members of the group may like to use this time of quietness to bring into the light of God's presence issues that they feel need further exploration. Use this time as an opportunity to tell others in the group of anything that has been particularly significant for you during the session, and pray about it together.

Further reflection on the theme of this session will be aided by using the readings for the week and the pattern of prayer outlined on pages 19–21. You may wish to use these, along with the words of praise and the meditation, as a group, or individually throughout the week.

PRAISE (BASED ON PSALM 27)

Leader: The Lord is my light and my salvation.
All: Whom shall I fear?
Leader: The Lord is my stronghold.
All: Whom shall I fear?
Leader: Be strong and take heart.
All: Of whom shall I be afraid?
Leader: The Lord is my light and my salvation.

> ### MEDITATION
> The moon is full tonight and the sea is calm.
> There is a pale reflection on the face of the deep —
> pieces of it break on the shore, sinking into the sand.
> Hours before, the beach was bathed in strong sunlight
> and the same sand scorched the soles of my feet.
>
> It is the same with the heart.
> Sometimes the light of God's presence
> gently ministers a healing touch
> in the calmness of the night.
> At other times the heat of that light scorches
> its message indelibly as though it were
> the height of noon.
>
> This candle burning before me now
> reminds me of that presence
> which, whether I turn to it or not, is always there.

Readings for the week

2 'I AM THE LIGHT OF THE WORLD'

Reflection	Day 5	Matthew 5:14–16: 'You are the light of the world'
	Day 6	2 Corinthians 4:1–6: Light shining in darkness
	Day 7	Ephesians 5:8–14: 'Children of light'

3 'I AM THE GOOD SHEPHERD'

Preparation	Day 1	Psalm 23: The Lord is my shepherd
	Day 2	Jeremiah 31:7–14: Gathering the flock
	Day 3	1 Samuel 17:32–37; Acts 20:28; 1 Peter 5:1–2: The shepherd's shepherd
Meeting	**Day 4**	**John 10:1–18: 'The good shepherd'**

3

'I AM THE GOOD SHEPHERD'

Aim

To see how we can follow Jesus' example of being a good shepherd.

Way in

During your times of reflection or preparation, has anything become particularly significant to you since the last meeting? Share it with the rest of the group, if you wish to.

PREPARING

If you wish, begin with music. Then spend time praying together.

Songs to sing

'Come, let us praise the Lord', MP 92.
'Come, let us worship', MP 97.
'O let the Son of God enfold you', MP 502, SHF 403, SOF 419.
'Shout for joy and sing', SOF 496.
'The King of love my Shepherd is', MP 649, SOF 533.
'The Lord's my Shepherd', MP 660, SOF 537.

Music to listen to

Beethoven: Symphony No 6 in F, Op 68 (Pastoral),
    4th movement, 'Shepherd's thanksgiving after the storm'.
Davy Spillane: 'Midnight Walker', from *Pipe Dreams*.

SHEPHERDING

To help you understand more fully the concept behind Jesus' statement, imagine what it would have been like to be a shepherd in first century Judea. What qualities do you think a good shepherd would have had?

Bible

Listen to the Bible passage as it is being read.

John 10:1–18

[Jesus said] [1] *'Very truly, I tell you, anyone who does not enter the sheepfold by the gate but climbs in by another way is a thief and a bandit.* [2] *The one who enters by the gate is the shepherd of the sheep.* [3] *The gatekeeper opens the gate for him, and the sheep hear his voice. He calls his own sheep by name and leads them out.* [4] *When he has brought out all his own, he goes ahead of them, and the sheep follow him because they know his voice.* [5] *They will not follow a stranger, but they will run from him because they do not know the voice of strangers.'* [6] *Jesus used this figure of speech with them, but they did not understand what he was saying to them.*

[7] *So again Jesus said to them, 'Very truly, I tell you, I am the gate for the sheep.* [8] *All who came before me are thieves and bandits; but the sheep did not listen to them.* [9] *I am the gate. Whoever enters by me will be saved, and will come in and go out and find pasture.* [10] *The thief comes only to steal and kill and destroy. I came that they may have life, and have it abundantly.*

[11] *'I am the good shepherd. The good shepherd lays down his life for the sheep.* [12] *The hired hand, who is not the shepherd and does not own the sheep, sees the wolf coming and leaves the sheep and runs away – and the wolf snatches them and scatters them.* [13] *The hired hand runs away because a hired hand does not care for the sheep.* [14] *I am the good shepherd. I know my own and my own know me,* [15] *just as the Father knows me and I know*

the Father. And I lay down my life for the sheep. [16] *I have other sheep that do not belong to this fold. I must bring them also, and they will listen to my voice. So there will be one flock, one shepherd.* [17] *For this reason the Father loves me, because I lay down my life in order to take it up again.* [18] *No one takes it from me, but I lay it down of my own accord. I have power to lay it down, and I have power to take it up again. I have received this command from my Father.'*

In biblical times a good shepherd was one who knew his sheep. He would recognise them both by their physical characteristics and by their personalities.

In the passage above, John speaks of the good shepherd whose voice is known by the flock. The shepherd calls his sheep by name and leads them out. He also:

Feeds his flock by providing them with good pasture and a supply of water.

Defends any of his flock who are attacked.

Cares for the flock, especially the weaker members.

Goes after those who stray and seeks to bring them back.

Provides a fold for the sheep as a protection against thieves and wild animals.

Makes sure the strong do not push the weak out of the fold.

Keeps guard at the entrance to the fold, since it has no physical gate.

As a group, discuss whether there are any parallels you can draw between the work of a good shepherd and the way in which Jesus shepherds his people. You may like to reflect on Psalm 23.

Life

You may find that the following questions help you explore what it means to be a good shepherd in today's world.

ME

'Keep watch over yourselves and over all the flock, of which the Holy Spirit has made you overseers, to shepherd the church of God that he obtained with the blood of his own Son' (Acts 20:28).

Are there individuals who act as shepherds for you (eg a church leader, a family member, a friend)?

Are there people for whom you take on a shepherding role?

CHURCH

'I exhort the elders among you to tend the flock of God that is in your charge, exercising the oversight, not under compulsion but willingly, as God would have you do it – not for sordid gain but eagerly. Do not lord it over those in your charge, but be examples to the flock. And when the chief shepherd appears, you will win the crown of glory that never fades away' (1 Peter 5:1b–4).

To what extent does the church live out Peter's instruction in the passage above?

What steps could you take to ensure that 'when the chief shepherd appears, you will win the crown'?

Response

As a group, share what you have discovered during the 'Life' section.

Prayer

People may want to give thanks for those who have shepherded them. Alternatively, they may wish to tell others in the group of the things that have been particularly significant for them during the session, and pray about them.

Further reflection on the theme of this session will be aided by using the readings for the week and the pattern of prayer outlined on pages 19–21. You may wish to use these, along with the words of petition and the meditation, as a group, or individually throughout the week.

PETITION (BASED ON PSALM 86)

Leader: Listen to me, Lord, and answer me.

All: For I am helpless and weak.

Leader: Listen to me, Lord, and answer me.

All: For I am your servant and I trust you.

Leader: Listen to me, Lord, and answer me.

All: For to you do I cry all day long.

Leader: O Lord my God, I will proclaim your faithfulness for ever. Teach me, Lord, what you want me to do. Teach me, O Lord my God, to serve you with complete devotion.

> MEDITATION
> Why should I pass through this gate
> with its narrow path, rough hewn timber,
> and very plain wood?
> It's just a few joints made by a carpenter.
> It is not appealing in the way
> that the ornate tracery of ironwork
> gleams a welcome to the grand, wide avenue
> over there.
> Why should I choose to follow this shepherd
> when so many are travelling that different road
> and seem very prosperous and happy in doing so?
> Perhaps it is because on the wide road
> there is no guide, just a crowd to follow.
> Whereas this shepherd knows who I am
> and was waiting to open the gate when I arrived.

Readings for the week

3 'I AM THE GOOD SHEPHERD'

Reflection	Day 5	Matthew 9:35–38: Being a shepherd
	Day 6	Luke 15:3–7: Searching for the sheep
	Day 7	John 21:15–17: 'Feed my sheep'

4 'I AM THE WAY, AND THE TRUTH'

Preparation	Day 1	Psalm 86:11–17: 'Teach me your way'
	Day 2	Psalm 25:4–10: 'Lead me in your truth'
	Day 3	Luke 7:24–28: Preparing the way
Meeting	**Day 4**	**John 14:1–4: 'I am the way, and the truth'**

4

'I AM THE WAY, AND THE TRUTH'

Aim

To explore the Christian way.

Way in

Those who wish to may share with the group any situation they have encountered during the previous week, in which someone's conduct played a particularly important part (eg seeing the truth being told in a difficult situation).

PREPARING

The songs below reflect the theme of this session. Allow time to pray together about the situations you have just discussed or about anything else individuals may wish to bring before God.

Songs to sing

'All the way my Saviour leads me', MP 22.
'Christ, the Way of life, possess me', MP 78.
'Do not be worried and upset', MP 117.
'How I love You', LP 69, MP 246, SHF 174, SOF 190.
'I will enter His gates', MP 307, SHF 252, SOF 268.
'Thou art the way', MP 695.

Music to listen to

Albinoni: Adagio in G minor for Strings and Organ.
Iona: 'Journey into the morn'.

MOVING ON

As a group or in pairs, look back over your Christian life. Can you see ways in which your attitude to people or to particular issues has changed or is changing?

Bible

Listen as the Bible passage is read.

John 14:1–14

[Jesus said] 1 *'Do not let your hearts be troubled. Believe in God, believe also in me.* 2 *In my Father's house there are many dwelling places. If it were not so, would I have told you that I go to prepare a place for you?* 3 *And if I go and prepare a place for you, I will come again and will take you to myself, so that where I am, there you may be also.* 4 *And you know the way to the place where I am going.'* 5 *Thomas said to him, 'Lord, we do not know where you are going. How can we know the way?'* 6 *Jesus said to him, 'I am the way, and the truth, and the life. No one comes to the Father except through me.* 7 *If you know me, you will know my Father also. From now on you do know him and have seen him.'*

8 *Philip said to him, 'Lord, show us the Father, and we will be satisfied.'* 9 *Jesus said to him, 'Have I been with you all this time, Philip, and you still do not know me? Whoever has seen me has seen the Father. How can you say, "Show us the Father"?* 10 *Do you not believe that I am in the Father and the Father is in me? The words that I say to you I do not speak on my own; but the Father who dwells in me does his works.* 11 *Believe me that I am in the Father and the Father is in me; but if you do not, then believe me because of the works themselves.* 12 *Very truly, I tell you, the one who believes in me will also do the works that I do and, in fact, will do greater works than these, because I am going to the Father.* 13 *I will do whatever you ask in my name, so that the Father may be glorified in the Son.* 14 *If in my name you ask me for anything, I will do it.'*

> REFLECTION
>
> The Christian way is one in which Jesus invites us to travel in his company, hand in hand with him. It is the way of deepening relationships. Jesus shows us this through his prayers to our Father in heaven – his prayers for his disciples and for us (John 17:6–26). The truth is that the way itself is prayer. Only as we pray do we move towards God, and only as we walk with Jesus do we grow in faith.

Luke 24:13

'Now on that same day two of [the disciples] were going to a village called Emmaus...'

Read and reflect on the meditation on page 42. (You may do this individually or as a group.)

What voices, images or ideas in the world around us do you think get in the way of hearing, seeing or understanding the truth Jesus teaches? Discuss this together as a group.

Life

THE WAY

Who are your spiritual companions (eg particularly close friends)?

> *continued on page 43*

MEDITATION

Can I travel the road alone,
or is it better that I share the journey
with this man who has offered to accompany me?
As we progress, he speaks of many things
I don't understand,
and some I have never thought about before.
And when he turns aside to pray, do I follow,
finding my own place apart, solitary yet not alone?

He says 'I tell you the truth' but I need help to hear it;
there are so many other voices I need to shut out.
He says 'I show you the truth' but I need help to see it;
there are so many other alluring images.
He says 'I will teach you the truth' but I need help
to understand it;
there are so many other conflicting ideas.
I ask what truth is,
and cannot see the answer is standing before me.

Now it is dusk, and we reach a resting place.
My companion makes to move on.
I press him to stay, knowing he will break bread —
then perhaps I will be able to recognise a truth
deeper than any he has yet revealed.

*Looking back, can you identify significant milestones,
(eg moments when you took important decisions to
change direction)?*

THE TRUTH

*Sometimes, even in the most ordinary conversation, we
get an unexpected revelation of truth. Can you think of
a time when this has happened to you, when you have
suddenly seen things in a totally new light?*

> *Has this revelation illuminated the way ahead (eg did it reveal something you needed to change, or give you reassurance)?*

Response

Spend time as a group sharing the things you discovered during the previous exercise.

Prayer

Use this time as an opportunity to tell others in the group of anything that has been particularly significant for you during the session, and pray about it together.

Further reflection on the theme for this session will be aided by using the readings for the week and the pattern of prayer outlined on pages 19–21. You may wish to use these, along with the words of petition below and the meditation on page 42, as a group, or individually throughout the week.

PETITION (BASED ON PSALM 40)
Leader: O Lord, I speak of your faithfulness.
All: May your love and your truth always protect me.
Leader: Do not withhold your mercy from me.
All: May your love and your truth always protect me.

Leader: Be pleased, O Lord, to save me.
All: **May your love and your truth always protect me.**
Leader: I waited patiently for the Lord and he heard me.

Readings for the week

4 'I AM THE WAY, AND THE TRUTH'

Reflection	Day 5	Isaiah 35: The way of holiness
	Day 6	Romans 11:33–36: 'Who has known the mind of the Lord?'
	Day 7	Colossians 1:3–14: The word of truth

5 'I AM THE RESURRECTION AND THE LIFE'

Preparation	Day 1	John 6:63–69: The Spirit gives life
	Day 2	2 Timothy 1:8–12: Death destroyed
	Day 3	2 Peter 3:11–18: Growing in grace
Meeting	**Day 4**	**John 11:25–27; 1 Peter 1:3–9: Revelation and life**

5

'I AM THE RESURRECTION AND THE LIFE'

Aim
To help us move further into 'life in all its fullness'.

Way in
Group members may like to share with each other the things that have become particularly significant to them during the preparation time leading up to today's session.

PREPARING
The songs listed below reflect the theme of this session. Spend time praying together.

Songs to sing
'All heaven declares', MP 14, SOF 10.
'And can it be', LP 8, MP 33, SHF 12, SHP 6, SOF 21.
'At your feet we fall', LP 10, MP 45, SHF 28, SOF 34.
'Breathe on me, Breath of God', LP 16, MP 67, SHF 47, SHP 11, SOF 51.
'Name of all majesty', LP 140, MP 481.
'O Breath of Life', MP 488, SHF 388, SHP 106, SOF 407.
'Thine be the glory', LP 233, MP 689, SHF 545, SHP 134, SOF 551.

Music to listen to
Allegri: 'Misere mei, Deus'.
Enya: 'How can I keep from singing', from *Shepherd Moons*.

THE FULLNESS OF LIFE

Do you feel you are living life in all its fullness? Invite people to share their feelings about this if they want to.

Bible

Listen as the Bible passages are read.

John 11:25–27

25 *Jesus said to [Martha], 'I am the resurrection and the life. Those who believe in me, even though they die, will live,* 26 *and everyone who lives and believes in me will never die. Do you believe this?'* 27 *She said to him, 'Yes, Lord, I believe that you are the Messiah, the Son of God, the one coming into the world.'*

1 Peter 1:3–9

3 *Blessed be the God and Father of our Lord Jesus Christ! By his great mercy he has given us a new birth into a living hope through the resurrection of Jesus Christ from the dead,* 4 *and into an inheritance that is imperishable, undefiled, and unfading, kept in heaven for you,* 5 *who are being protected by the power of God through faith for a salvation ready to be revealed in the last time.* 6 *In this you rejoice, even if now for a little while you have had to suffer various trials,* 7 *so that the genuineness of your faith – being more precious than gold that, though perishable, is tested by fire – may be found to result in praise and glory and honour when Jesus Christ is revealed.* 8 *Although you have not seen him, you love him; and even though you do not see him now, you believe in him and rejoice with an indescribable and glorious joy,* 9 *for you are receiving the outcome of your faith, the salvation of your souls.*

The person speaking in the following three meditations is Jesus. Try to imagine the surroundings and the sensations he is describing. If you are in a group, one person may like to read the meditation slowly, pausing from time to time to give others the opportunity to focus on what is happening.

MEDITATION 1
The villa in Cana is a beautiful place,
cool and welcoming at this time of year.
I enjoy visiting my friends here,
and what better than for the wedding of two of them.
It looks as if the whole town has turned out —
it's almost impossible to get in.
Now the steward is telling my mother something
about the wine running out,
and she is looking at me.
Why do I have to be involved?
I'm a carpenter, not a wine merchant.
But her eyes contain the message
I sensed was coming.
I didn't expect it to be her
or now...

MEDITATION 2
I come to bring understanding,
to open hearts and minds to the reality
of the new life in my Father's kingdom,
to raise anew those whose lives have been deadened
by the hopelessness of sin.
I come, as the prophet said, to loose the captive
and to give sight to the blind.
I am called Master, Rabbi, Teacher,
and rightly so, for I am all of these,
and yet I am more...

> **MEDITATION 3**
> It is a hot, dry day.
> The crowds gathered early when they heard
> I was coming.
> It's almost impossible to move,
> there are so many people.
> I'm being pushed forward,
> regardless of whether I want to go or not.
> Suddenly I know I have been touched
> by someone's faith,
> and in all that crowd
> I see one pair of eyes
> which reach my heart...

In these meditations we encounter Jesus as friend, teacher, healer. How might it feel to be Jesus in these situations? Discuss this together as a group.

Life

In the following visualisation, imagine again what it might be like to be Jesus. Then look at your own expectations, hopes and fears.

> Sometimes it is wonderful just to get away
> from the stress and pressure of it all.
> So many people, so much pain.
> So many expectations, so much hope and fear.
> It is necessary to be among them
> but also to find the place apart
> in which I can meet with my Father who is in heaven.
> I look for the wild places, the high places,
> the quiet places,
> knowing that then I can be solitary,
> yet never alone...

Where do you go in order to find God and release the pressure? Where for you are the places where you can be 'solitary, yet never alone'? You may like to use the layout below.

EXPECTATIONS

HOPES

FEARS

PLACES APART
(Solitary, yet never alone.)

Response

As a group, talk about what you have discovered from the previous exercise.

Prayer

Use this time as an opportunity to tell others in the group anything that has been particularly significant for you during the session, and pray about it together.

Further reflection on the theme for this session will be aided by using the readings for the week and the pattern of prayer outlined on pages 19–21. You may wish to use these, along with the words of petition and the meditation, as a group, or individually throughout the week.

PETITION (BASED ON PSALM 16)

Leader: Keep me safe O God.

All: **In you I find my rest.**

Leader: Lord, you have made me secure.

All: **In you I find my rest.**

Leader: You have made known to me the path of life.

All: **In you I find my rest.**

Leader: My heart is glad, for you will not abandon me.

> MEDITATION
> Here in the dark, dry stillness of the tomb
> lies the silence that has no voice.
> It is the same silence that surrounds all the things
> gathered in my home before I enter
> at the end of a long day.
> The silent gods among my possessions
> say nothing about me.
> They merely hint at my needs and pretensions.
> When I enter a room, I bring life to the things I use,
> but this life does not last beyond my presence.

> *continued*

The cup I drink from may reveal something of the
contents it once held,
but can say nothing of the one who used it.

What I seek is life which lasts beyond the present,
which is not defeated by the silence of the tomb,
which knows in whom it resides.

I must take off the old self and put on the new.
I can only do this through the one
who offers me resurrection
through his lifting me to new life
in his name and service.

He removes the grave clothes of the world
and opens the way to new life in eternity.

Readings for the week

5 'I AM THE RESURRECTION AND THE LIFE'

Reflection	Day 5	Psalm 16: The path of life
	Day 6	1 Timothy 6:11–16: Fight the good fight
	Day 7	1 John 5:1–13: Eternal life

6 'I AM THE VINE'

Preparation	Day 1	Isaiah 5:1–7: The vineyard of the Lord
	Day 2	Matthew 7:15–23: The tree and its fruit
	Day 3	Matthew 21:33–41: The owner of the vineyard
Meeting	**Day 4**	**John 15:1–11: 'I am the vine'**

6

'I AM THE VINE'

Aim

To help us understand better what it means to be 'in Jesus'.

Way in

Reflecting on the last session, has anything emerged which has prompted you to take a new approach to an aspect of your life? Talk about this for a few minutes with another member of the group.

PREPARING

As before, you may like to begin with some music. The following songs reflect the theme of this session. Take time to pray together.

Songs to sing

'Come, let us sing', MP 94, SHF 67, SOF 72.
'I am the Bread', MP 260.
'I have a destiny', SOF 212.
'We shall stand', LP 217, MP 737, SOF 589.
'You are the Vine', MP 792, SHF 633, SOF 629.

Music to listen to

Vaughan Williams: 'The Lark Ascending'.
J S Bach: Prelude from Suite No 1 in G for cello.

LIFE IN JESUS

The great privilege of the Christian life is that we can rely on Jesus to sustain us (see the reading below). How do you feel this is worked out in your daily life? Ask people to suggest one or two examples.

*B*ible
Listen as the Bible passage is read.

John 15:1–11

[Jesus said] [1] 'I am the true vine, and my Father is the vinegrower. [2] He removes every branch in me that bears no fruit. Every branch that bears fruit he prunes to make it bear more fruit. [3] You have already been cleansed by the word that I have spoken to you. [4] Abide in me as I abide in you. Just as the branch cannot bear fruit by itself unless it abides in the vine, neither can you unless you abide in me. [5] I am the vine, you are the branches. Those who abide in me and I in them bear much fruit, because apart from me you can do nothing. [6] Whoever does not abide in me is thrown away like a branch and withers; such branches are gathered, thrown into the fire, and burned. [7] If you abide in me, and my words abide in you, ask for whatever you wish, and it will be done for you. [8] My Father is glorified in this, that you bear much fruit and become my disciples. [9] As the Father has loved me, so I have loved you; abide in my love. [10] If you keep my commandments, you will abide in my love, just as I have kept my Father's commandments and abide in his love. [11] I have said these things to you so that my joy may be in you, and that your joy may be complete.'

The vine grower's art relies heavily on selecting the right young vines to graft into the strongest root stock. The new branch is cut from its own roots and placed in a V-shaped groove channelled in the vine. The grafted branch is bound in place until it is completely integrated. Later, as it grows and fruits, it is pruned by the vinedresser to keep it healthy and fruitful. A branch that does not bear fruit is removed completely.

MEDITATION

Is this a step I am prepared to take,
this giving up of the roots which have served me
until now?
For all my years, my family, these people, this place
have provided my security
and given me a space and some meaning.
Now I face an alternative —
my family will now be this fellowship I join.
I will belong where I am sent or called to be.
My meaning will come from the awareness of myself
discovered in this new reality.
'Trust me,' he says.
'My Father will cut your roots away
and graft you into me.'

In your life, what has it meant to be 'grafted into the vine'? How
has your view of the world changed since you committed yourself
to being 'bound to Christ'?

Life

Proof of the effectiveness of the new branch is its fruitfulness.

Galatians 5:22–23
> *The fruit of the Spirit is love, joy, peace, patience, kindness, generosity, faithfulness, gentleness, and self-control. There is no law against such things.*

Looking back, can you see areas of your life:

* which have been / are being pruned?
* which have borne / are bearing fruit?

(You may like to use the chart below to make notes.)

PRUNING

(eg cutting back on excesses like overwork, bad habits, attitudes)

BEARING FRUIT

(eg greater patience, self-control)

Response

Share as much as you wish of your findings with the group.

Prayer

Use this time as an opportunity to tell others in the group of anything that has been particularly significant for you during the session, and pray about it together.

Further reflection on the theme for this session will be aided by using the readings for the week and the pattern of prayer (pages 19–21). You may wish to use these, along with the words of praise and the meditation (page 59), as a group, or individually throughout the week.

PRAISE (BASED ON PSALM 139)

Leader: O Lord, you have searched me and you know me.
All: You laid your hand upon me.
Leader: You created my inmost being.
All: You laid your hand upon me.
Leader: When I was made in the secret place...
All: You laid your hand upon me.
Leader: O Lord, you have searched me and you know me.

Readings for the week

6 'I AM THE VINE'

Reflection	Day 5	Romans 7:4–6: The new way
	Day 6	Philippians 1:3–11: The fruit of righteousness
	Day 7	1 John 3:11–24: Life in Christ

THROUGH THE BIBLE
IN A YEAR

A beautiful gift book which helps the reader to work their way through the whole Bible in a year while recording their spiritual journey.

Eleven themes, linking Old and New Testament passages, vividly present the overarching story of the Bible. Clear introductions to the themes, brief commentary on the unfolding story, and a thought, prayer or quote for each week, enhance the journal format which provides space for the reader to record their response each day.

1 85999 196 3
£9.99

Available from Christian bookshops or direct from Scripture Union on 01865 716880

LIFEBUILDER BIBLE STUDIES

LifeBuilder Bible study guides have helped millions of individuals dig deeper into the Bible. The series contains over 50 titles, most based on Bible books and some on biblical themes.
Price £2.99 each

Acts	Loving Justice
Angels	Luke
Christian Beliefs	Mark
Christian Character	Mary
Christian Disciplines	Meeting God
1 Corinthians	Meeting Jesus
2 Corinthians	Meeting the Spirit
Daniel	New Testament Characters
David	Old Testament Characters
Ecclesiastes	Parables
Ephesians	Philippians
Esther	Prayer
Evangelism	Proverbs
Exodus	Psalms
Faith	Psalms II
Fruit of the Spirit	Revelation
Galatians	Romans
Genesis	Self Esteem
Hebrews	Sermon on the Mount
Hope	Small Group Starter Kit
Hosea	Spiritual Gifts
James	Ten Commandments
Jeremiah	Women of the New Testament
Job	Women of the Old Tesatment
John's Gospel	
Jonah, Joel, Amos	
Judges	
Love	

Available from Christian bookshops or direct from Scripture Unoin on 01865 716880.